PIANO • VOCAL • GUITAR

Christmas with Disney

Disney characters and artwork © Disney Enterprises, Inc.

ISBN 978-1-4768-1269-4

WALT DISNEY MUSIC COMPANY
WONDERLAND MUSIC COMPANY, INC.

HAL•LEONARD®
CORPORATION

7777 W. BLUEMOUND RD. P.O. BOX 13819 MILWAUKEE, WI 53213

Visit Hal Leonard Online at
www.halleonard.com

Christmas with Disney

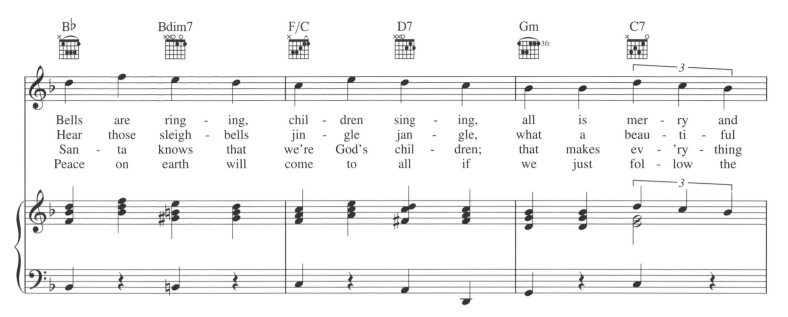

Bells are ring - ing, chil - dren sing - ing, all is mer - ry and
Hear those sleigh - bells jin - gle jan - gle, what a beau - ti - ful
San - ta knows that we're God's chil - dren; that makes ev - 'ry - thing
Peace on earth will come to all if we just fol - low the

bright. Hang your stock - ings and say your pray'rs,
sight. Jump in bed, cov - er up your head, } 'cause
right. Fill your hearts with a Christ - mas cheer,
light. Let's give thanks to the Lord a - bove,

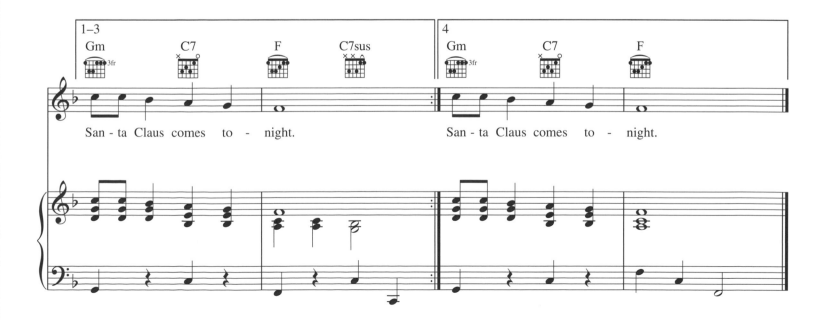

San - ta Claus comes to - night.   San - ta Claus comes to - night.

THE TWELVE DAYS OF CHRISTMAS

Traditional English Carol

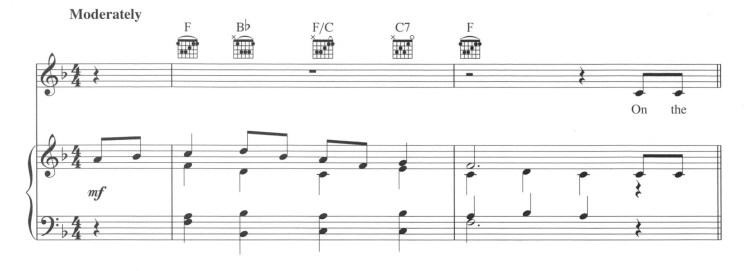

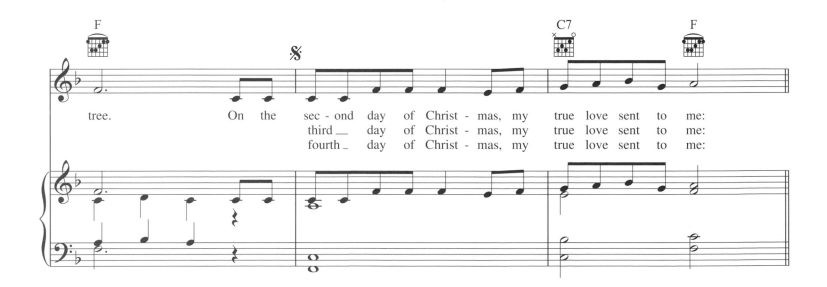

Two tur - tle - doves,
Three French ___ hens,
Four call - ing birds,
and a par - tridge ___ in a pear

tree. On the tree. On the fifth day of Christ - mas, my

true love sent to me: Five gold ___ rings!

Four ___ call - ing birds, three French hens, two ___ tur - tle - doves, and a

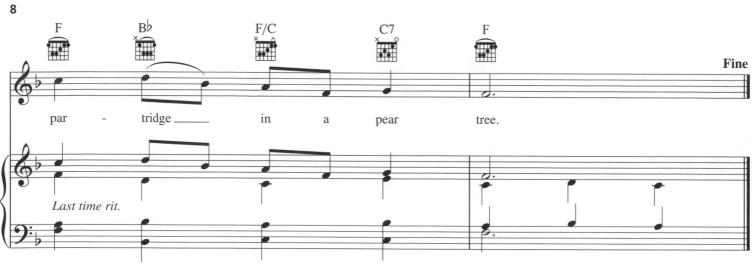

Fine

par - tridge _____ in a pear tree.

Last time rit.

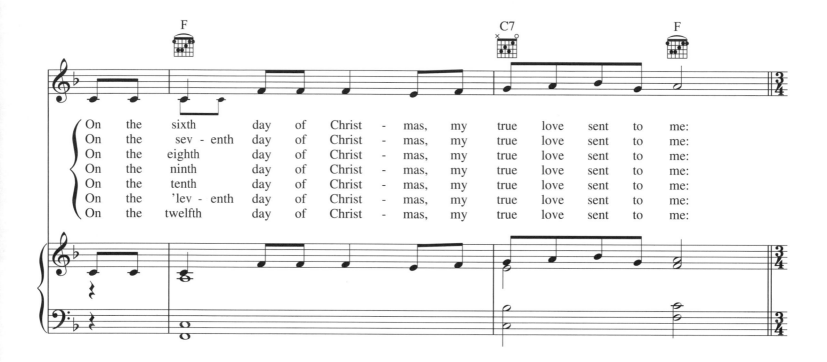

On the sixth day of Christ - mas, my true love sent to me:
On the sev - enth day of Christ - mas, my true love sent to me:
On the eighth day of Christ - mas, my true love sent to me:
On the ninth day of Christ - mas, my true love sent to me:
On the tenth day of Christ - mas, my true love sent to me:
On the 'lev - enth day of Christ - mas, my true love sent to me:
On the twelfth day of Christ - mas, my true love sent to me:

Repeat as needed

D.S.S
(Last time D.S.S. al Fine)

Six ____ geese a - lay - ing,
Sev - en swans a - swim - ming,
Eight ____ maids a - milk - ing,
Nine ____ la - dies danc - ing,
Ten ____ lords a - leap - ing,
'Lev - en pip - ers pip - ing,
Twelve ____ drum - mers drum - ming,

five gold _____ rings!

JINGLE BELLS/
SLEIGH RIDE THROUGH THE SNOW

Traditional
Arranged by RICHARD FRIEDMAN

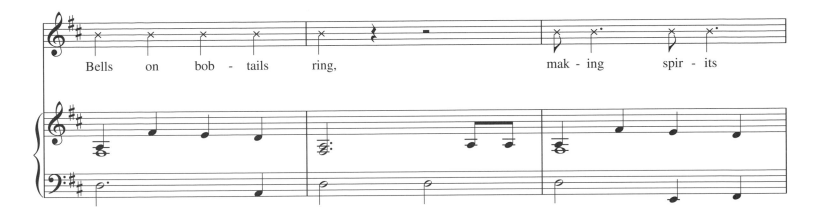

Bells on bob - tails ring, mak - ing spir - its

bright. What fun it is to ride and sing a sleigh - ing song to -

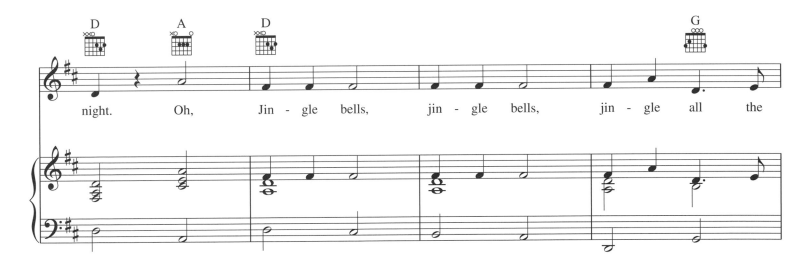

night. Oh, Jin - gle bells, jin - gle bells, jin - gle all the

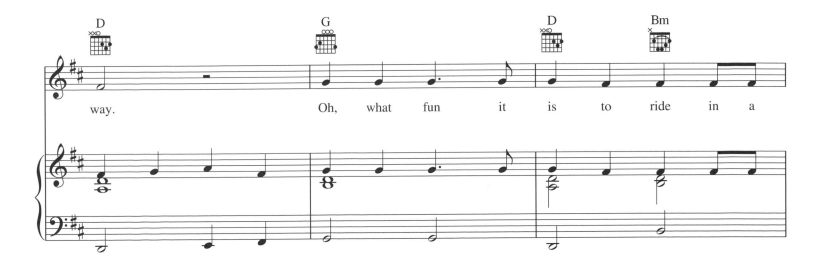

way. Oh, what fun it is to ride in a

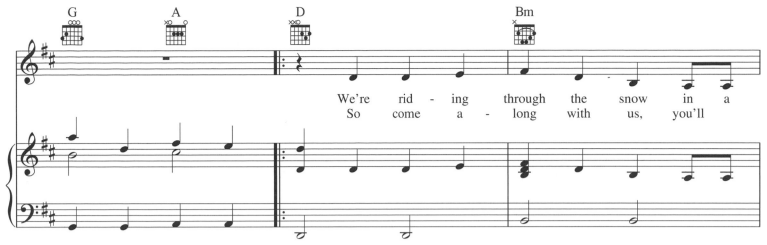

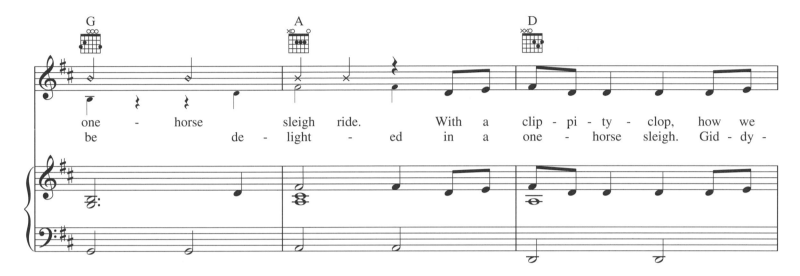

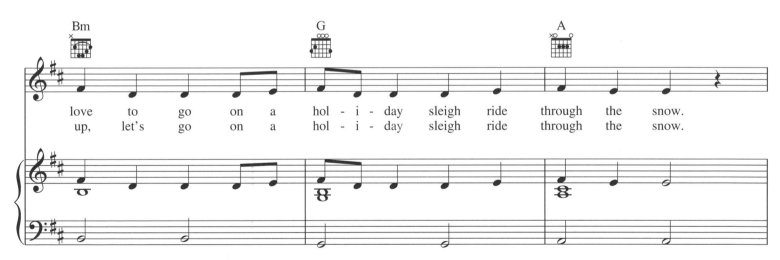

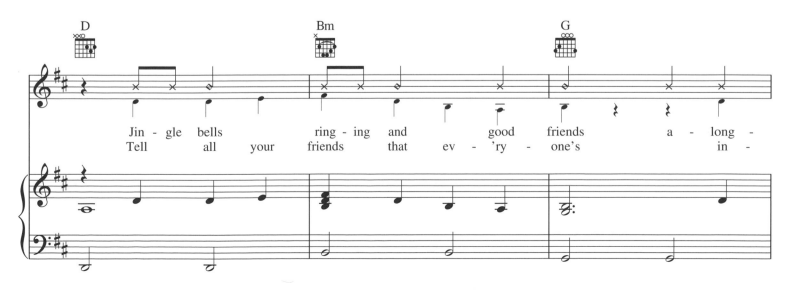

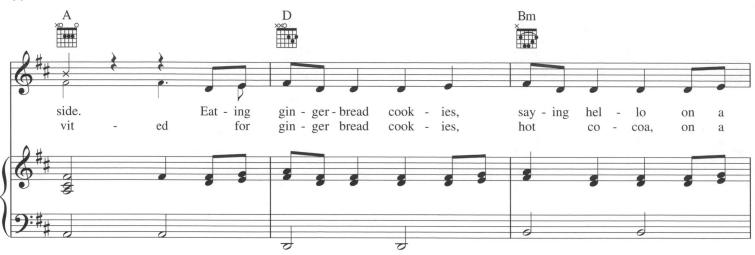

side. Eat - ing gin - ger - bread cook - ies, say - ing hel - lo on a
vit - ed for gin - ger bread cook - ies, hot co - coa, on a

hol - i - day sleigh ride through the snow. We'll turn down
hol - i - day sleigh ride through the snow. And now we'll

San - ta Claus Lane and sing some Christ - mas car - ols.
make this ride a hol - i - day tra - di - tion.

We'll laugh the whole day through, 'cause it's the
Each year, we'll wait for you,

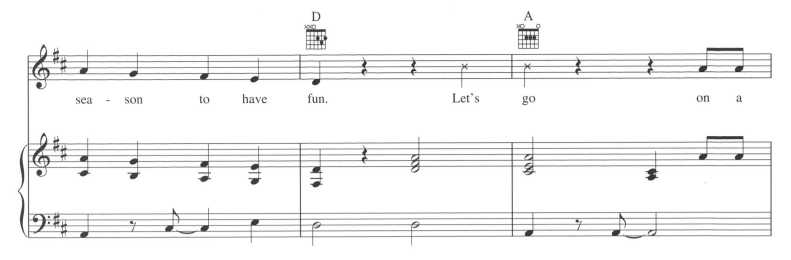

sea - son to have fun. Let's go on a

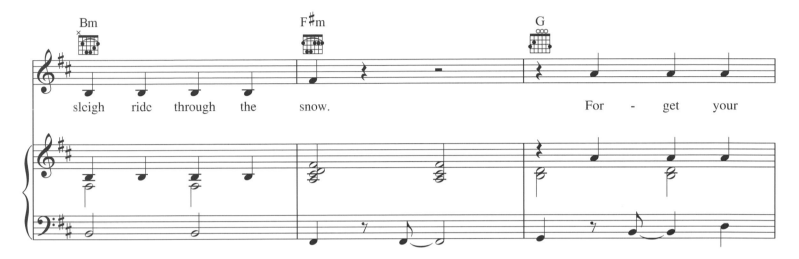

sleigh ride through the snow. For - get your

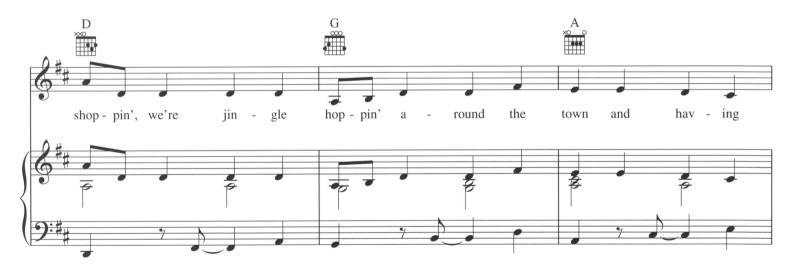

shop - pin', we're jin - gle hop - pin' a - round the town and hav - ing

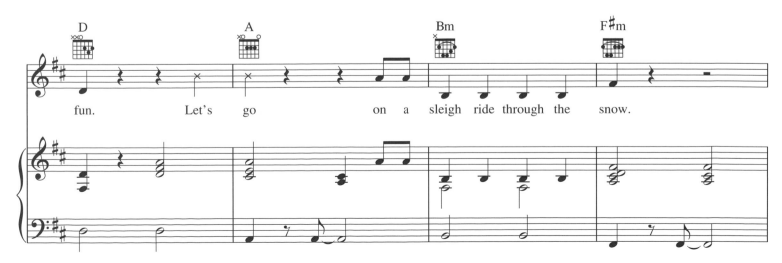

fun. Let's go on a sleigh ride through the snow.

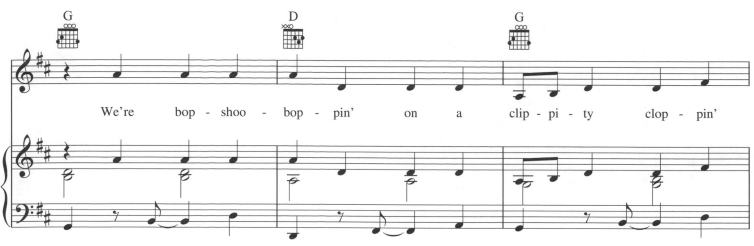

We're bop - shoo - bop - pin' on a clip - pi - ty clop - pin'

sleigh ride through the snow.

Jin - gle bells, jin - gle bells,
snow.

jin - gle all the way. We're bop - shoo -

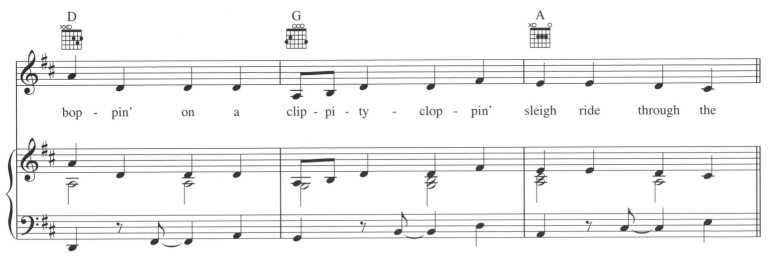

bop - pin' on a clip - pi - ty - clop - pin' sleigh ride through the

Jin - gle bells, jin - gle bells, jin - gle all the
snow. way.

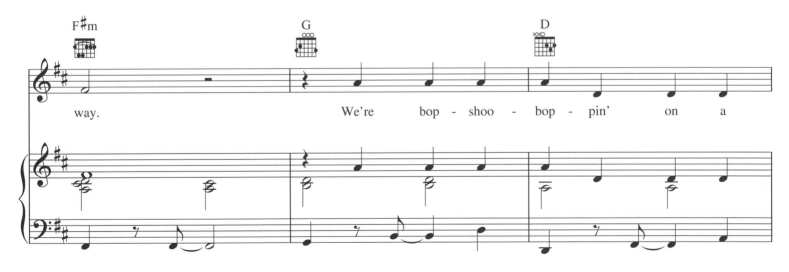

We're bop - shoo - bop - pin' on a

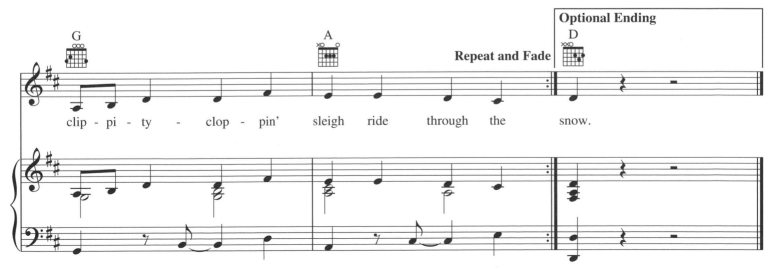

clip - pi - ty - clop - pin' sleigh ride through the snow.

RUDOLPH THE RED-NOSED REINDEER

Music and Lyrics by
JOHNNY MARKS

Lyrics:

You know Dash-er and Danc-er and Pranc-er and Vix-en,

Com-et and Cu-pid and Don-ner and Blitz-en, but do you re-

call the most fa-mous rein-deer of all?

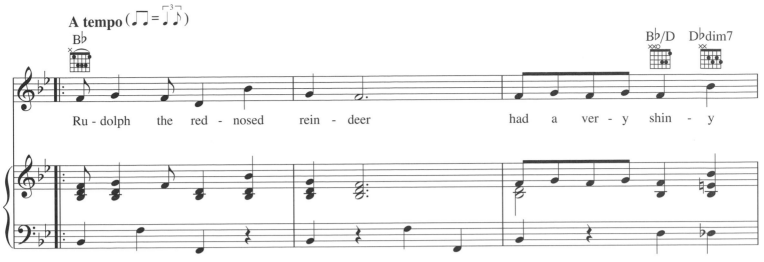

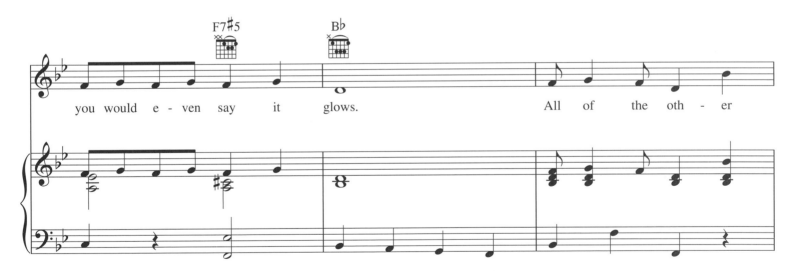

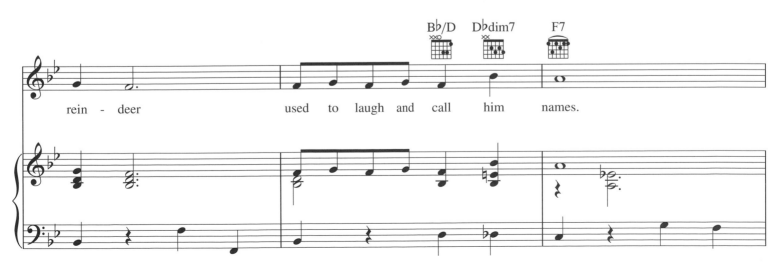

They nev - er let poor Ru - dolph join in an - y rein - deer

games. Then one fog - gy Christ - mas Eve,

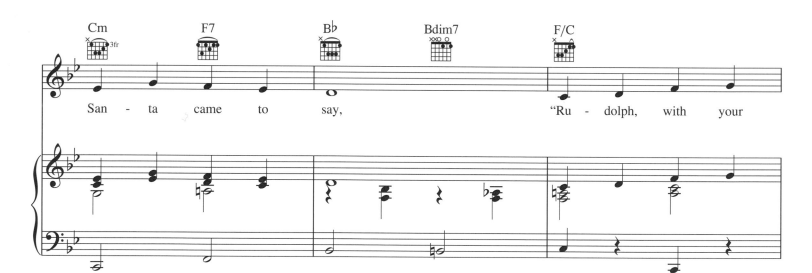

San - ta came to say, "Ru - dolph, with your

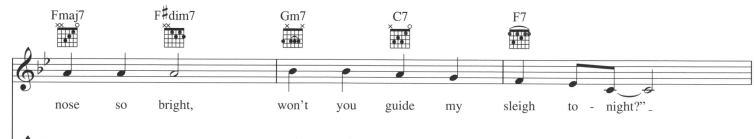

nose so bright, won't you guide my sleigh to - night?"

Then how the rein - deer loved him, as they shout - ed out with

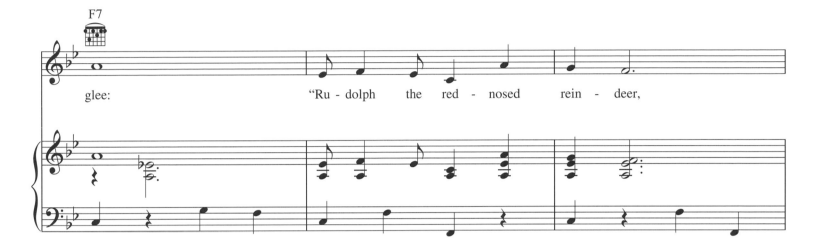

glee: "Ru - dolph the red - nosed rein - deer,

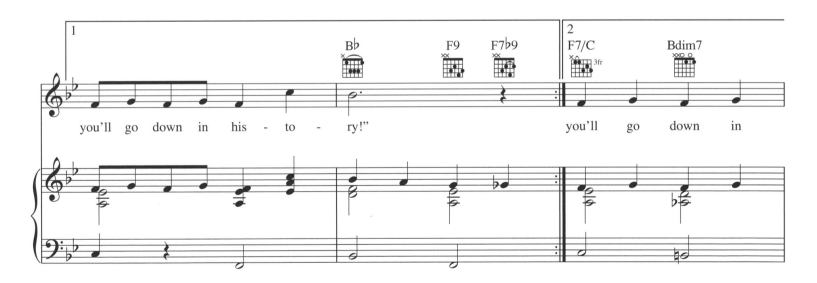

you'll go down in his - to - ry!" you'll go down in

his - to - ry!" _____

FROSTY THE SNOW MAN

Words and Music by STEVE NELSON
and JACK ROLLINS

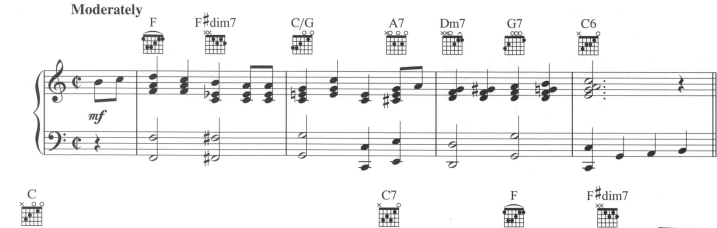

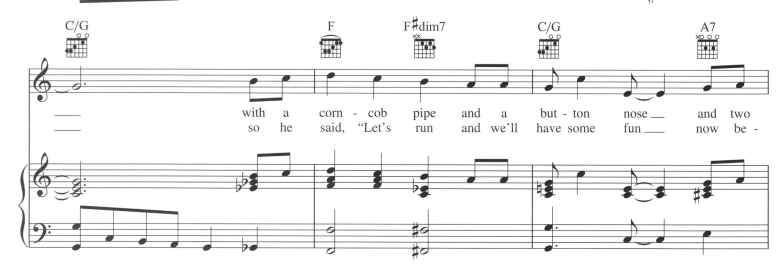

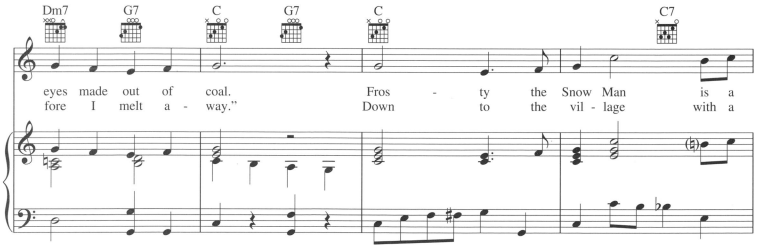

fair - y tale, they say; _____ he was made of snow but the
broom - stick in his hand, _____ run - ning here and there all a -

chil - dren know __ how he came to life one day. There
round the square __ say - in', "Catch me if you can." He

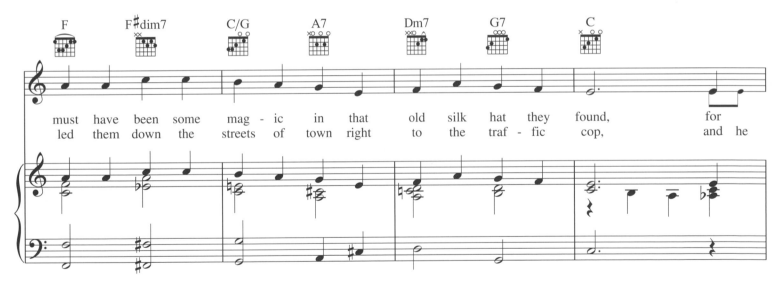

must have been some mag - ic in that old silk hat they found, for
led them down the streets of town right to the traf - fic cop, and he

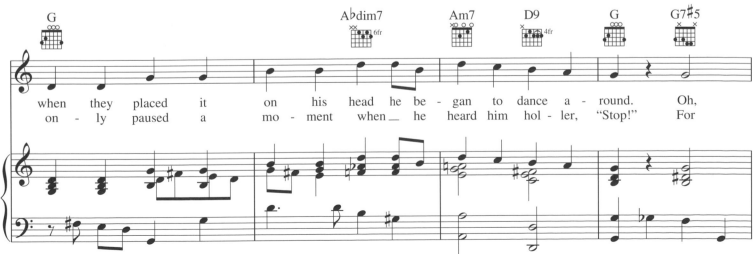

when they placed it on his head he be - gan to dance a - round. Oh,
on - ly paused a mo - ment when __ he heard him hol - ler, "Stop!" For

SLEIGH RIDE

Music by LEROY ANDERSON
Words by MITCHELL PARISH

Just hear those sleigh bells jin-gle-ing, ring-ting-tin-gle-ing, too. ____ Come on, it's love-ly weath-er for a sleigh ride to-geth-er with you. ____

love-ly weath-er for a sleigh ride to-geth-er with you. _____ There's a

birth-day par-ty at the home of Farm-er Gray. It-'ll
hap-py feel-ing noth-ing in the world can buy, when they

be the per-fect end-ing of a per-fect day. We'll be
pass a-round the cof-fee and the pump-kin pie. It-'ll

sing-ing the songs we love to sing with-out a sin-gle
near-ly be like a pic-ture print by Cur-ri-er and

HERE WE COME A-CAROLING

Traditional
Arranged by RICHARD FRIEDMAN

Lilting Folk

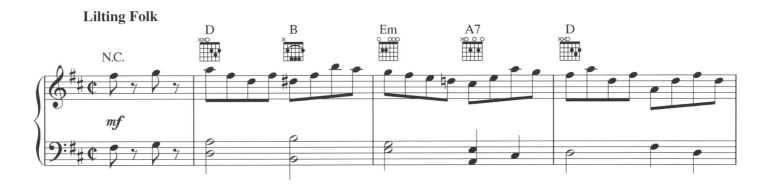

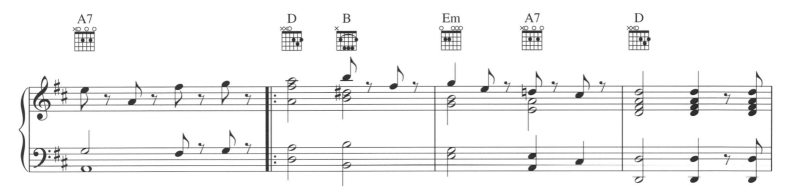

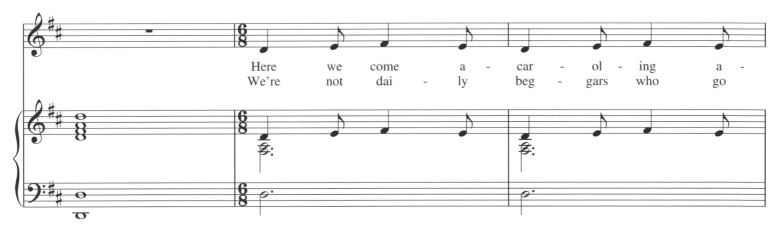

Here we come a - car - ol - ing a -
We're not dai - ly beg - gars who go

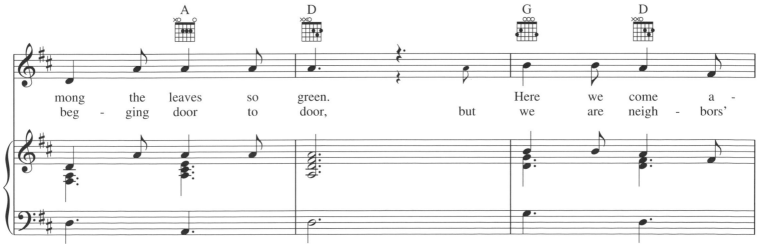

mong the leaves so green. Here we come a -
beg - ging door to door, but we are neigh - bors'

wan - d'ring, so fair _____ to be seen. Love and
chil - dren, whom you have seen be - fore.

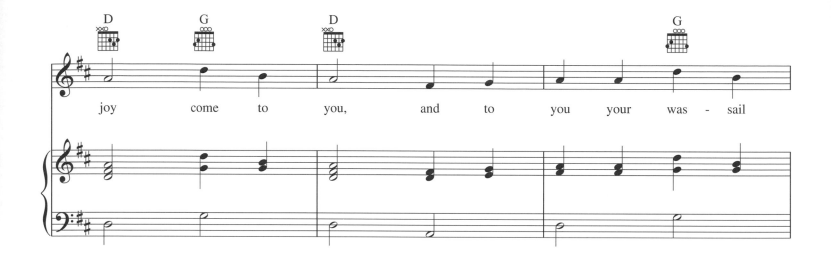

joy come to you, and to you your was - sail

too. And God bless you and send _____ you a

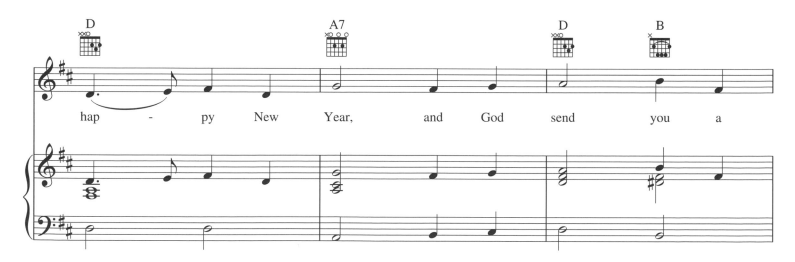

hap - py New Year, and God send you a

hap - py New Year.

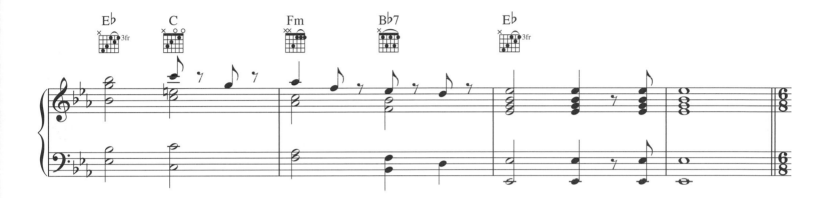

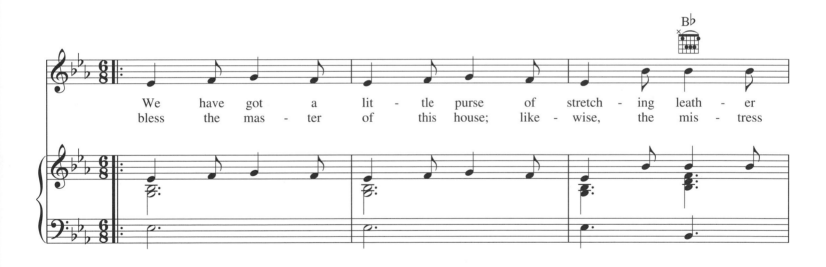

We have got a lit - tle purse of stretch - ing leath - er
bless the mas - ter of this house; like - wise, the mis - tress

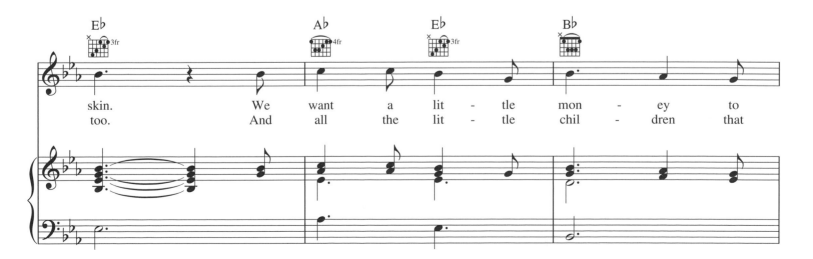

skin. We want a lit - tle mon - ey to
too. And all the lit - tle chil - dren that

line it well with- in.
'round the ta - ble in go.
Love and joy come to

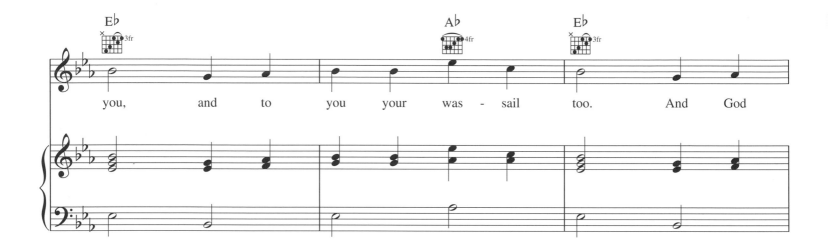

you, and to you your was - sail too. And God

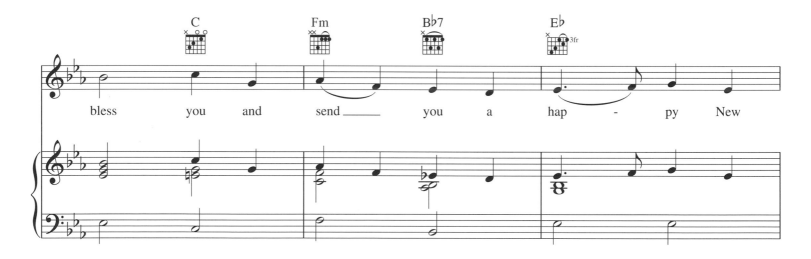

bless you and send_____ you a hap - py New

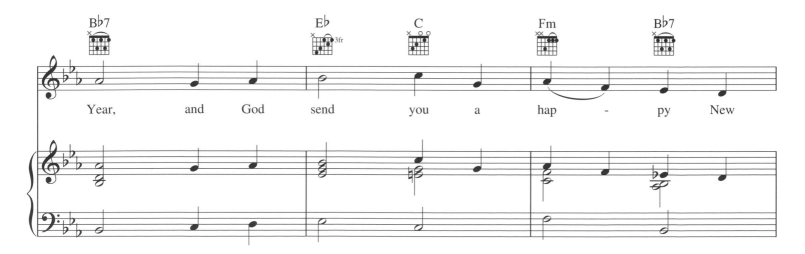

Year, and God send you a hap - py New

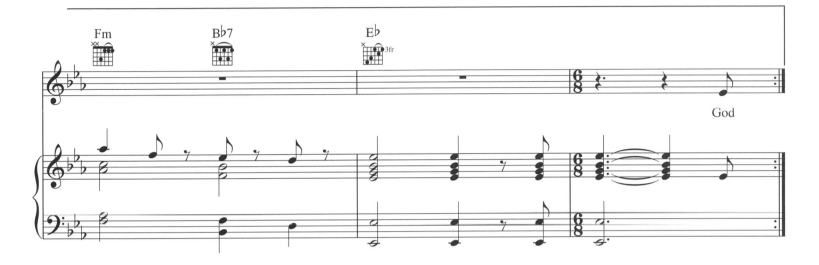

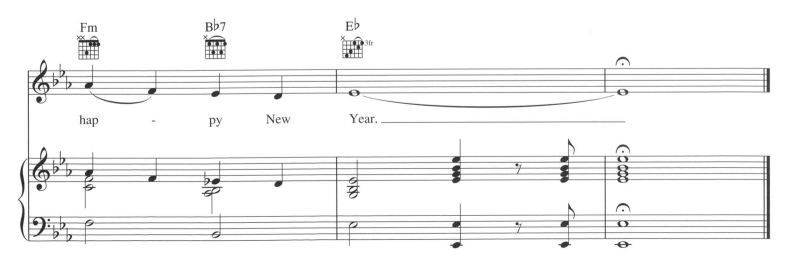

DECK THE HALLS

Traditional
Additional Lyrics by ROBIN FREDERICK

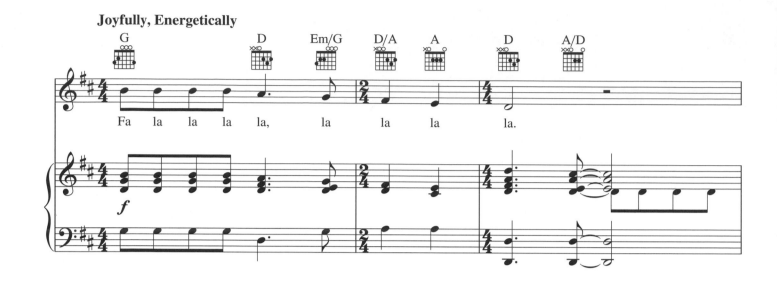

Joyfully, Energetically

Fa la la la la, la la la la la.

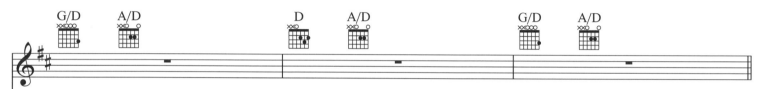

Spoken: It's time to open up the Christmas stockings! Yay! That's a fine idea.

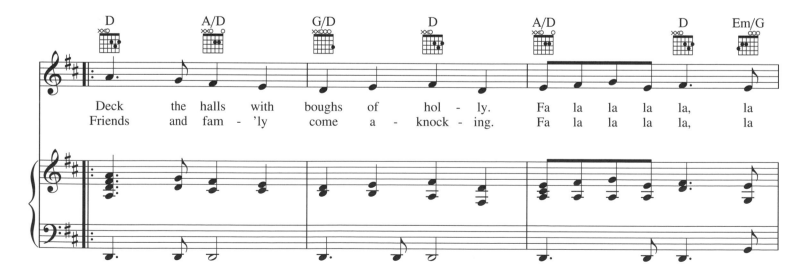

Deck the halls with boughs of hol - ly. Fa la la la la, la
Friends and fam - 'ly come a - knock - ing. Fa la la la la, la

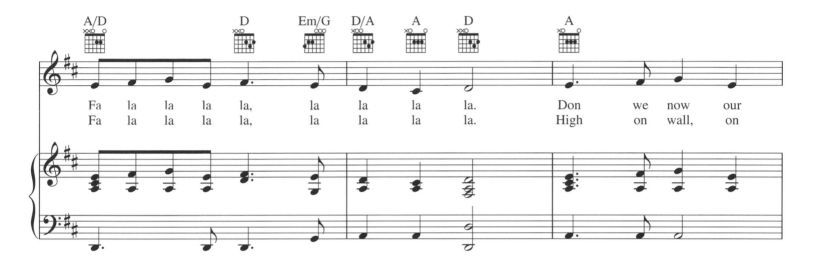

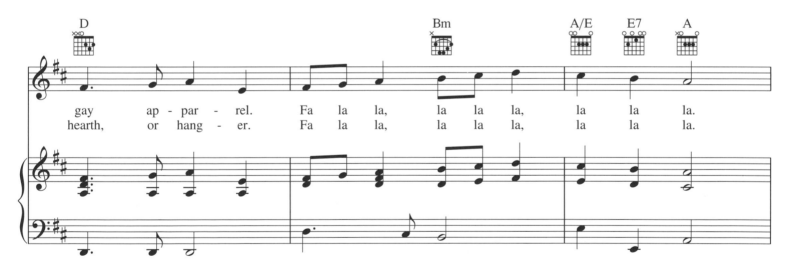

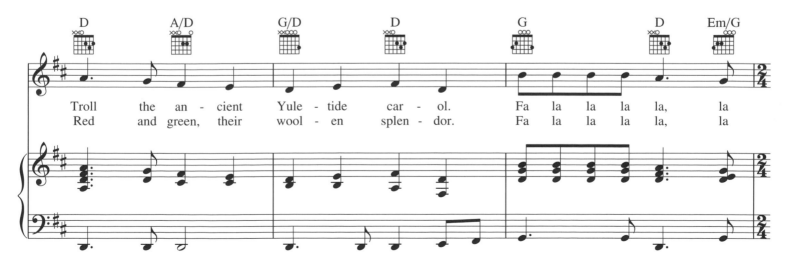

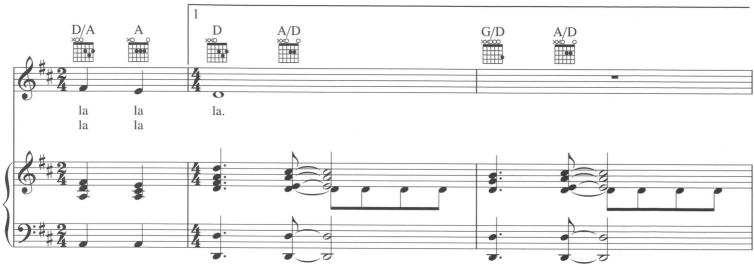

la la la.
la la

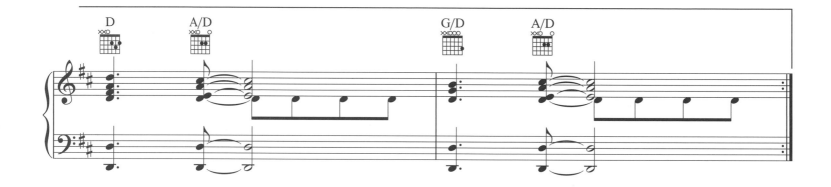

la.

And now, laddies, here's a nice Christmas stocking for each one of you.

This one says "Huey". And this one is Dewey's. And Louie. And this one is Donald's.

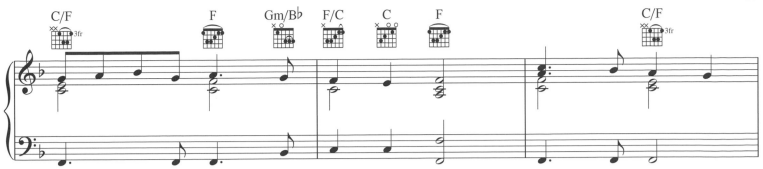

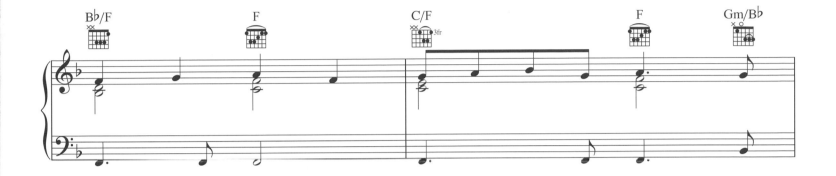

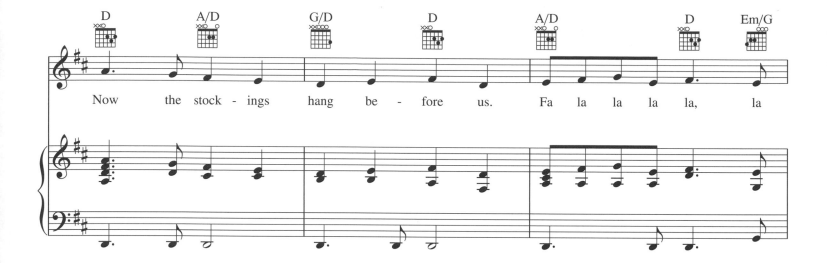

Now the stock - ings hang be - fore us. Fa la la la la, la

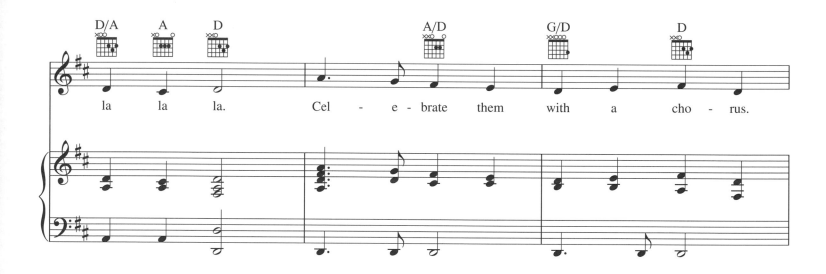

la la la. Cel - e - brate them with a cho - rus.

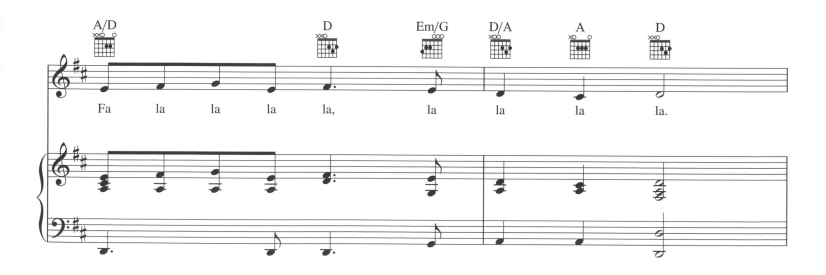

Fa la la la la, la la la la.

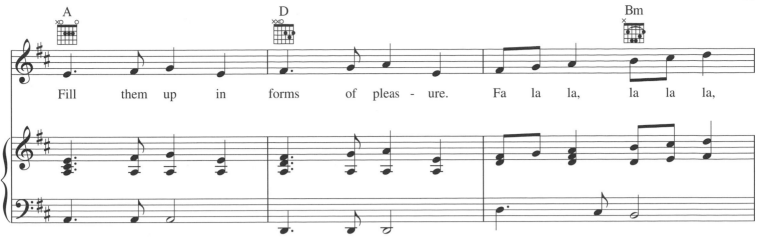

Fill them up in forms of pleas - ure. Fa la la, la la la,

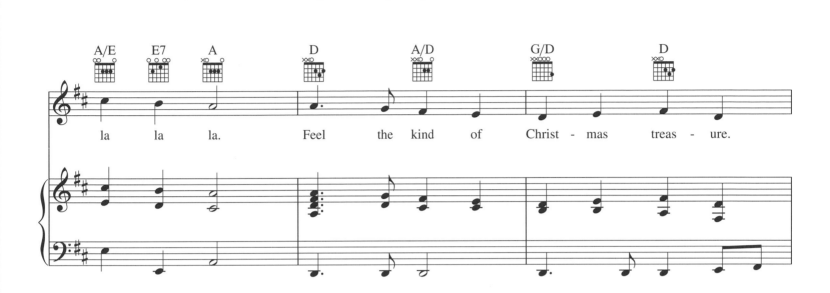

la la la. Feel the kind of Christ - mas treas - ure.

Fa la la la la, la la la la. Fa la la la la, la

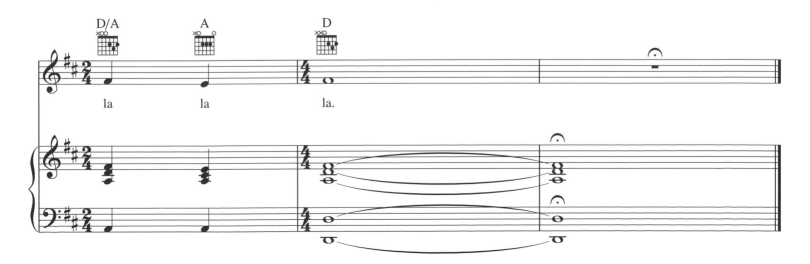

la la la.

JOY TO THE WORLD

Words by ISAAC WATTS
Music by GEORGE FRIDERIC HANDEL
Arranged by LOWELL MASON

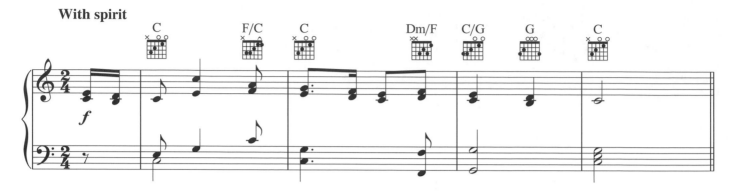

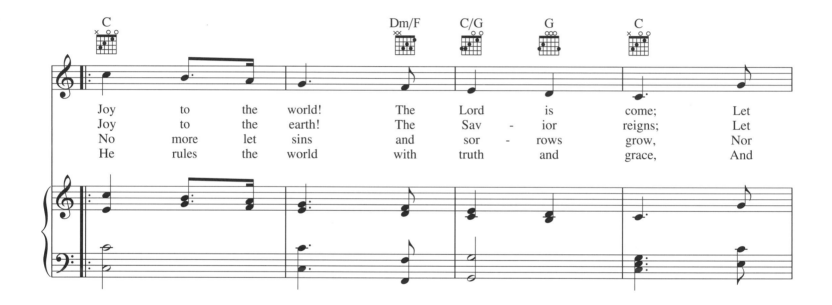

Joy to the world! The Lord is come; Let
Joy to the world! The earth! The Sav - ior reigns; Let
No more let sins and sor - rows grow, Nor
He rules the world with truth and grace, And

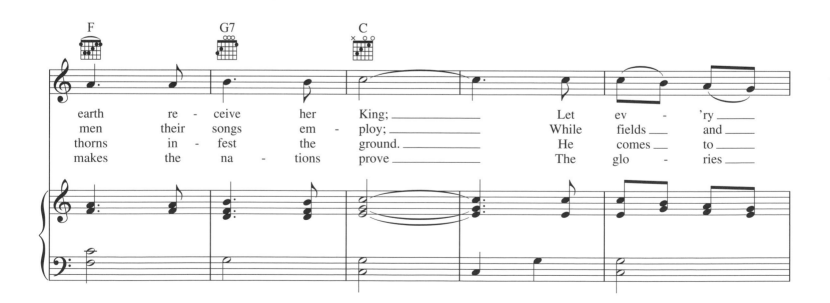

earth re - ceive her King; _____ Let ev - 'ry _____
men their songs em - ploy; _____ While fields ___ and ___
thorns in - fest the ground. _____ He comes ___ to ___
makes the na - tions prove _____ The glo - ries _____

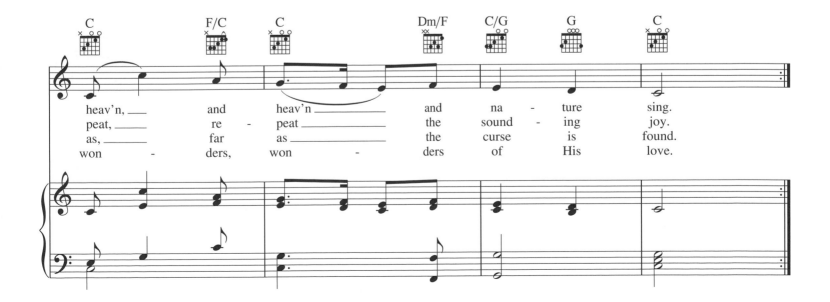

JOLLY OLD ST. NICHOLAS

Traditional 19th Century American Carol

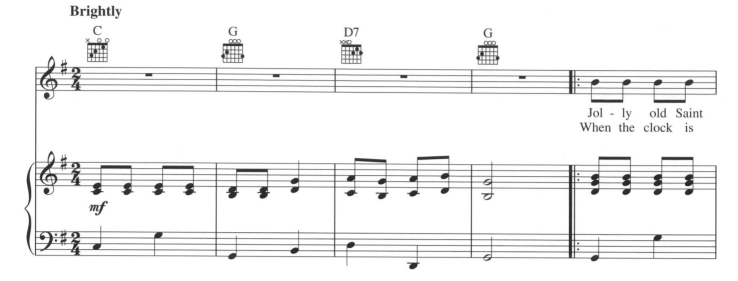

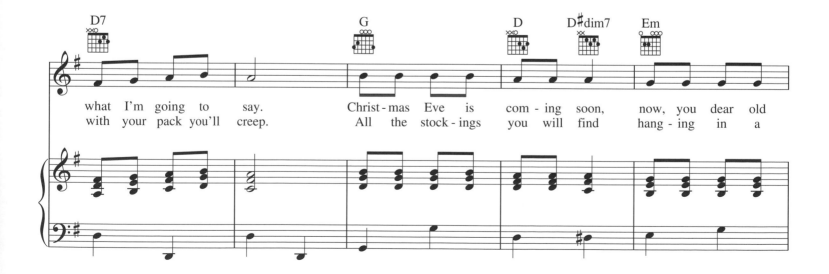

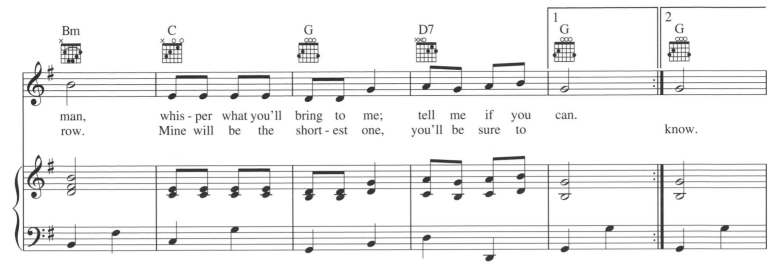

man, whis-per what you'll bring to me; tell me if you can.
row. Mine will be the short-est one, you'll be sure to know.

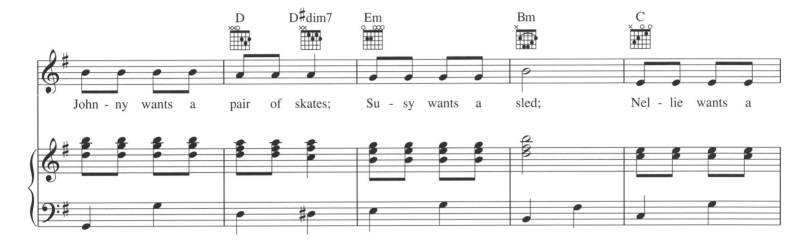

John - ny wants a pair of skates; Su - sy wants a sled; Nel - lie wants a

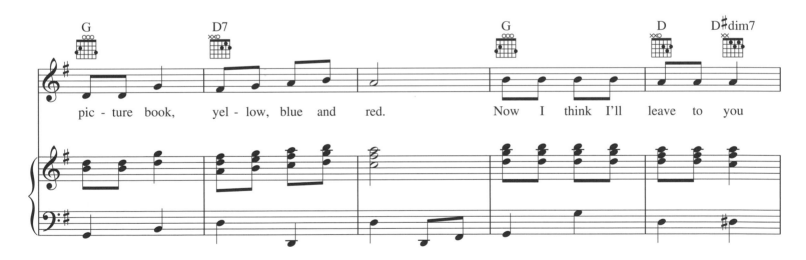

pic - ture book, yel - low, blue and red. Now I think I'll leave to you

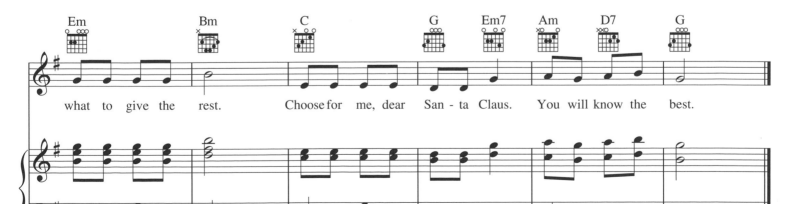

what to give the rest. Choose for me, dear San - ta Claus. You will know the best.

SILENT NIGHT

Words by JOSEPH MOHR
Translated by JOHN F. YOUNG
Music by FRANZ X. GRUBER

AWAY IN A MANGER

Words by JOHN T. McFARLAND (v.3)
Music by JAMES R. MURRAY

A - way in a man - ger, no crib for a bed, The

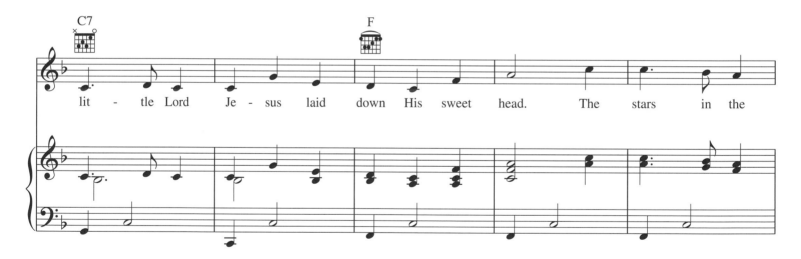

lit - tle Lord Je - sus laid down His sweet head. The stars in the

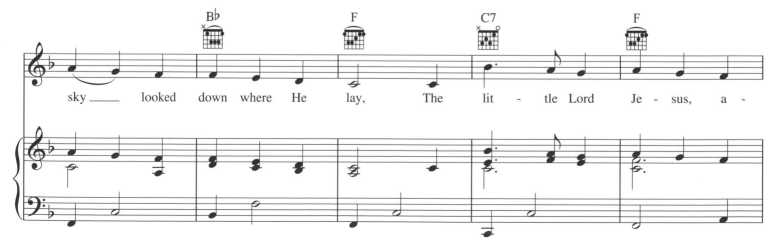

sky ___ looked down where He lay, The lit - tle Lord Je - sus, a -

sleep on the hay. The cat - tle are low - ing, the ba - by a -

wakes, But lit - tle Lord Je - sus, no cry - ing He

makes. I love Thee, Lord Je - sus, look down from the

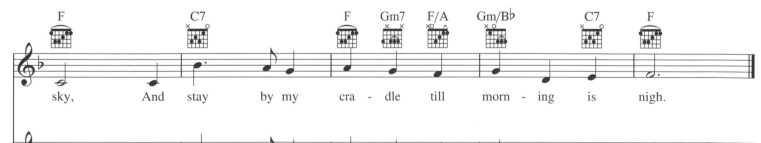

sky, And stay by my cra - dle till morn - ing is nigh.

CHRISTMAS TOGETHER/
O CHRISTMAS TREE

Words and Music by
PHILIP BARON

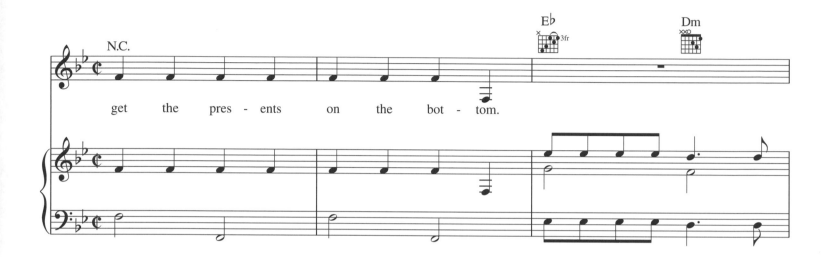

got 'em.   I'll put the star up - on the top. _____ And don't for -

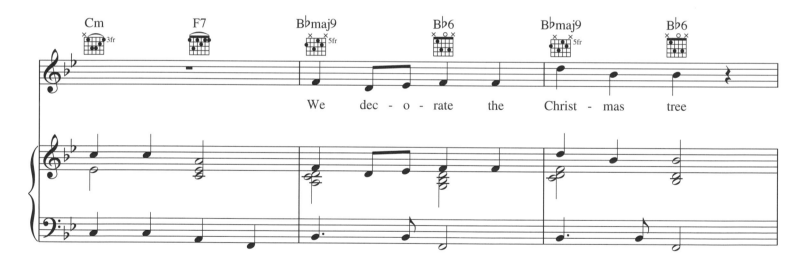

get the pres - ents on the bot - tom.

We dec - o - rate the Christ - mas tree

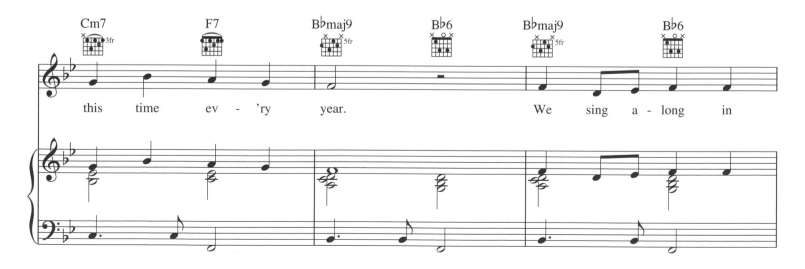

this time ev - 'ry year.   We sing a - long in

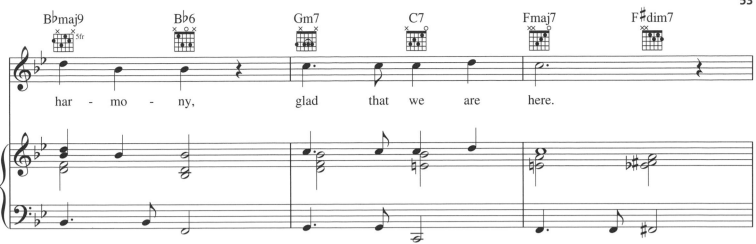

har-mo-ny, glad that we are here.

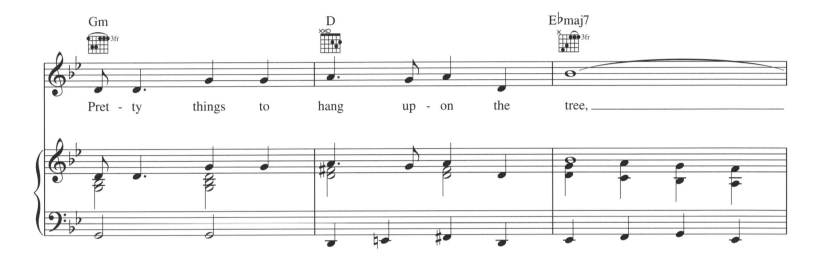

Pret-ty things to hang up-on the tree, _____

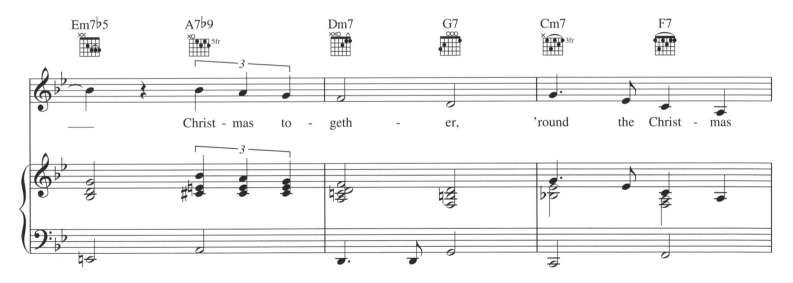

_____ Christ-mas to-geth-er, 'round the Christ-mas

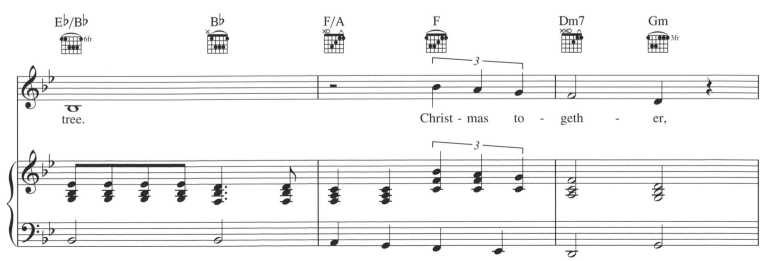

tree. Christ-mas to-geth-er,

O CHRISTMAS TREE

Traditional
Additional Lyrics by ROBIN FREDERICK

Slower, choral

Christ-mas tree, O Christ-mas tree, how love-ly are your branch-es. O
Christ-mas tree, O Christ-mas tree, how love-ly are your branch-es. Your
shin-ing star and twink-ling lights, they gent-ly glow through-out the night. O
Christ-mas tree, O Christ-mas tree, how love-ly are your branch-es.

SANTA CLAUS IS COMIN' TO TOWN

Words by HAVEN GILLESPIE
Music by J. FRED COOTS

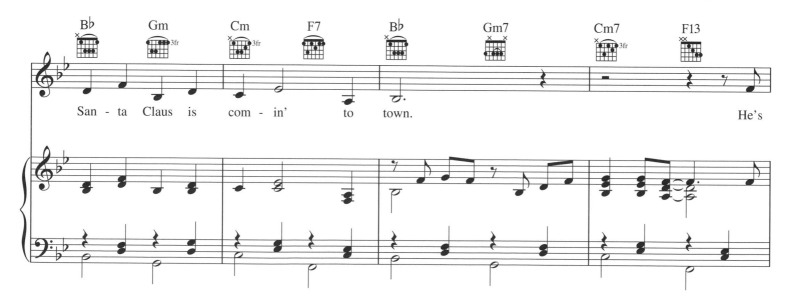

FROM ALL OF US TO ALL OF YOU

Lyrics by GIL GEORGE
Music by PAUL J. SMITH

gath - er 'round our love - ly tree, where all the lights are shin - ing. We'll

be as hap - py as can be, while all the bells are chim - ing.

Ab   Eb   Ab   Eb

Ding,   dong,   din - gle,   what a mer - ry sound.
Haha, hi, folks! Merry Christmas!   Hap - py New Year, too.

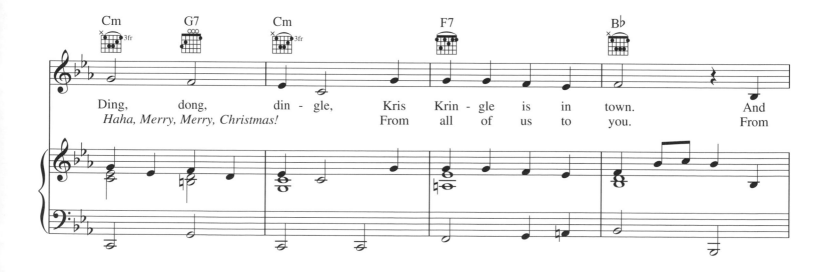

Cm   G7   Cm   F7   Bb

Ding,   dong,   din - gle,   Kris Krin - gle is in town. And
Haha, Merry, Merry, Christmas!   From all of us to you. From

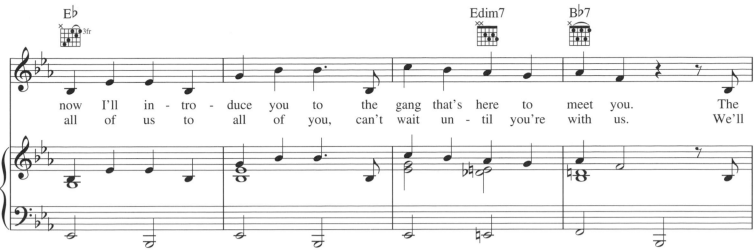

now I'll in-tro-duce you to the gang that's here to meet you. The
all of us to all of you, can't wait un-til you're with us. We'll

hap - py house of Mick-ey Mouse is wait - ing here to greet you.

wait be - neath the mis - tle - toe and say a Mer - ry

Christ - mas.

WE WISH YOU A MERRY CHRISTMAS

Traditional
Arranged by RICHARD FRIEDMAN

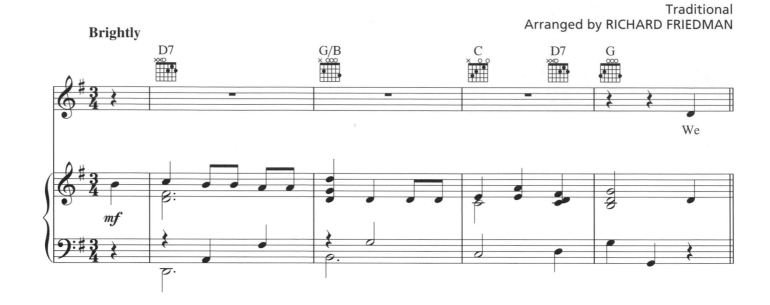

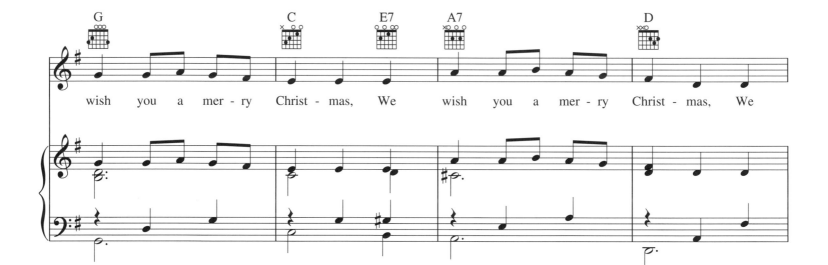

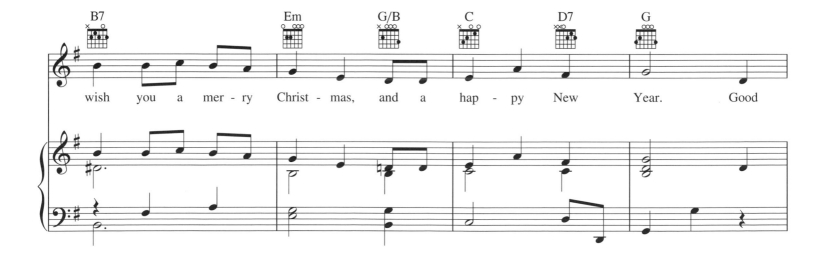

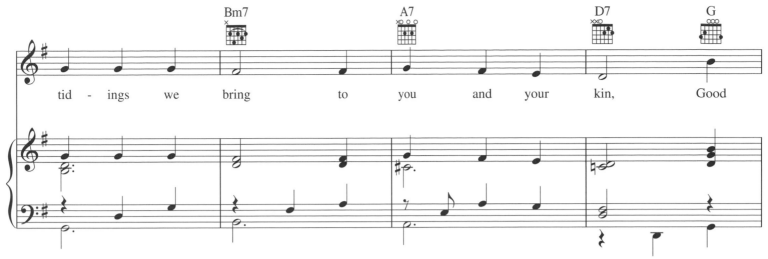

tid - ings we bring to you and your kin, Good

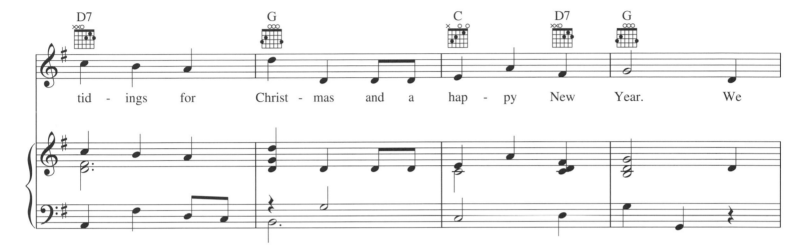

tid - ings for Christ - mas and a hap - py New Year. We

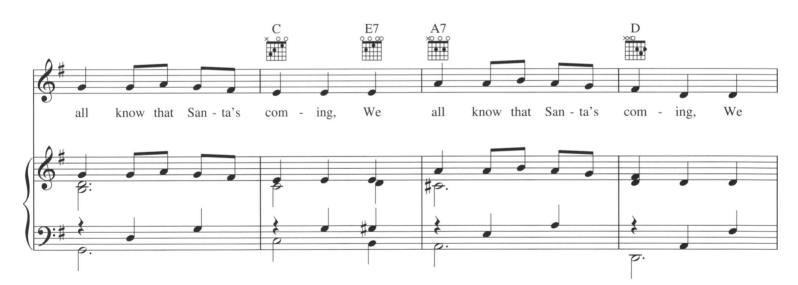

all know that San - ta's com - ing, We all know that San - ta's com - ing, We

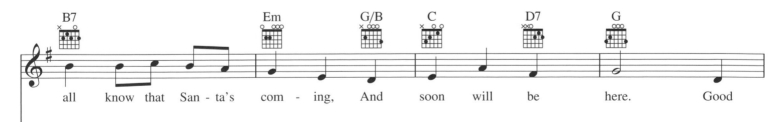

all know that San - ta's com - ing, And soon will be here. Good

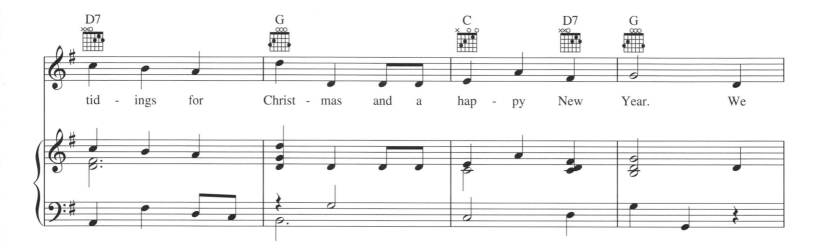

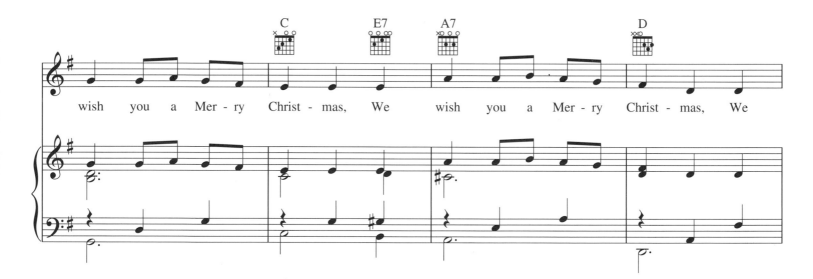

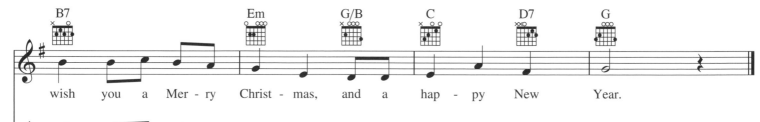